# S U S H I

 A Headlands Press Book

# S U S H I

Mia Detrick

Photographs by Kathryn Kleinman

Chronicle Books    San Francisco

Produced by The Headlands Press, Inc., Tiburon, California; Andrew Fluegelman, producer

Editor: Susan Brenneman
Art director/designer: Michael Patrick Cronan
Sushi preparation: Takemi Kimura
Food stylist: Sara Slavin
Photographer's assistant: Selina Jones
Mechanical production: Shannon Terry, Debi Shimamoto
Illustrations: Shannon Terry

Composed in Bembo on a Mergenthaler VIP by Robert Sibley
Printed and bound by Dai Nippon Printing Co., Ltd., Tōkyō, Japan

Library of Congress Cataloging in Publication Data

Detrick, Mia.
    Sushi.

    Includes index.
    1. Cookery (Fish) 2. Sushi. I. Kleinman, Kathryn. II. Title.
    TX747.D47    641.6'92    81-12224
    ISBN 0-87701-238-5    AACR2

10 9 8 7 6 5

*For Sumi*

After my first astonishing taste of flying-fish roe and quail egg, I went looking for a book on the art of eating sushi. Finding none, I decided to write one myself and I spent the next months touring sushi bars from Los Angeles to Vancouver, quizzing dozens of chefs on the mysteries of this intoxicating cuisine. Their generosity was boundless, and the more I learned about sushi, the more I discovered that it was just a reflection of the vast intricacies of the Japanese culture, and the more I had to learn. Along the way, my affection for the Japanese and their culture all but surpassed my passion for sushi.

# ACKNOWLEDGMENTS

I am indebted to many people for the time and expertise they contributed to this book. My special thanks go to Sumi Hasegawa Jacobs of Sushi Gen in Sausalito, California, who has been a friend and an unrelenting teacher of the subtleties and wisdom of Japanese culture; to Takemi Kimura, head chef at Sushi Gen, who prepared the exquisite food for the photographs in this book, painstakingly reviewed the manuscript through a translator, and taught me the meaning of Japanese grace, composure, and craftsmanship; and to Keiji Hiyama, head sushi chef at Yamato in San Francisco, who did his best to teach me in a few weeks what it took him a decade to learn.

Thanks also to the many sushi chefs who answered my questions while they fed and entertained me. In particular, chefs Ippei Nishimura and Goro Kato of Kansai in San Francisco, Yoshi Taguchi of Sushi Gen, Fumio Ishii of Fuku Sushi in San Francisco, and Hideo Inomata of Restaurant Ino in Mill Valley, California.

Many others contributed their knowledge and resources to this book, and their help is also greatly appreciated. Mitsuru Akashi, manager of Nikko in San Francisco; Koichi Inagaki of the San Francisco office of the Japan Food Corporation; and Tomio Iwamoto, Department of Ichthyology, California Academy of Sciences, San Francisco, all aided in the research. Mako Hachiska provided invaluable aid by translating and reviewing the manuscript. Asakichi Sakakibara added immeasurably to the photographs by providing antique artifacts from his San Francisco store, Asakichi. Dr. Isaac Kikawada of the University of California at Berkeley helped solve language problems. And chef Aki Kawata of Sushi Gen created the beautiful festival sushi for our photograph.

All the people at Sushi Gen, who opened their beautiful restaurant to me, deserve particular thanks for doing so much to make this book happen.

The talented people who made this book beautiful did it out of love, and my gratitude to them can never be adequately expressed. Thanks to Kathryn Kleinman for the exquisite photographs, to Michael Patrick Cronan for book design, to Sara Slavin for food styling and pulling everything together, to Susan Brenneman for editing the manuscript, and to Andrew Fluegelman for producing this book in record time.

Finally, a special thanks to my staff at Peaches and Cream and at Smith's Greenhouse in Mill Valley, who kept the home fires burning in my absence.

—M.D.

# CONTENTS

A Japanese proverb says that if you have the pleasant experience of eating something you have not tasted before, your life will be lengthened by seventy-five days. One evening at a sushi bar could add years to your life.

Sushi is the aristocrat of snack food and worthy of being a meal in itself. The most perfect fish and shellfish are served uncooked in gemlike portions with a delicately seasoned rice. An engaging chef prepares your order in front of you, with flair and precision, and presents it with a graciousness as satisfying as the beautiful food itself. Sushi bars are lively, congenial places, and you are likely to be drawn into conversation with other people at the counter, or share a sake with the chef. The camaraderie, the sake, the purity of the food, and its theatrical presentation combine to inspire a heady phenomenon some call sushi rapture.

Not too long ago, few Americans had tasted sushi, or wanted to. On their way into Japanese restaurants, they hurried past the sushi bar with eyes averted, avoiding what seemed an indecent display of raw fish and octopus legs. Americans have been characteristically suspicious of raw fish. They expect it to taste "fishy," or be slippery and unpleasant. Ironically, many people who recoil at the thought of eating raw fish gleefully swallow raw oysters, and there is nothing quite so raw as an oyster.

Clearly, only a supremely delightful cuisine could overcome such obstacles. Devotees describe their fondness for sushi as an addiction, and the recent proliferation of sushi bars in the United States is evidence that sushi is a cuisine whose time has come.

The starring attraction of the sushi bar is fresh raw seafood fastidiously selected and prepared, served as *sashimi*, sliced and beautifully arranged; as *nigirizushi*, sliced and pressed on a small pad of lightly vinegared rice; or as *makizushi*, rolled up in vinegared rice and crisp seaweed and cut into bite-sized chunks. Anything other than sushi, sashimi, tea, and sake is considered irrelevant at a sushi bar, and this intense focus is reflected in the perfection of the food.

# INTRODUCTION

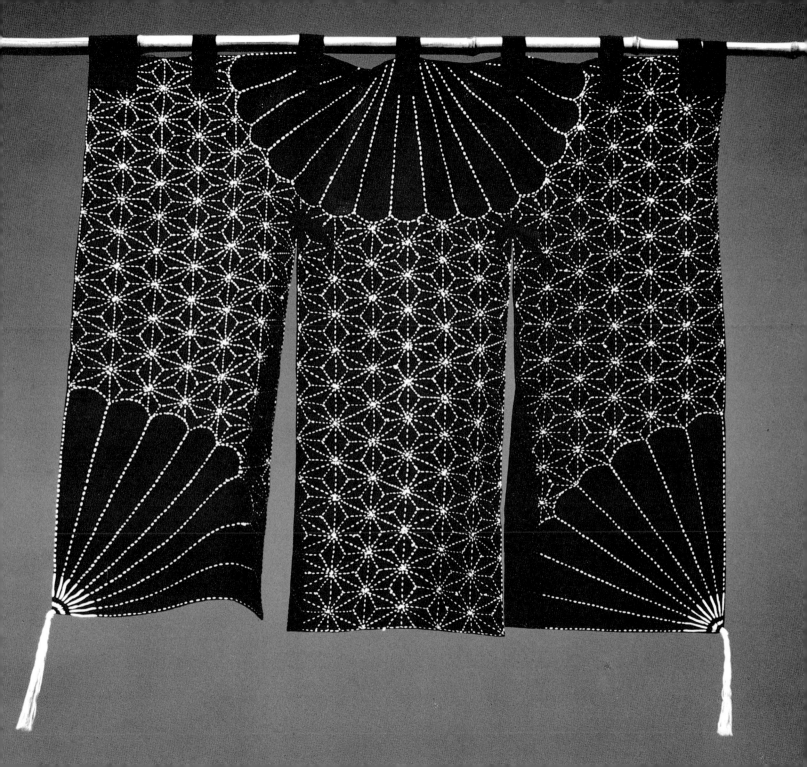

At first you may be a bit tentative about trying some of the delicacies displayed in the sushi case. Sushi chefs are remarkably attuned to their customers' tastes and experience, and if you explain you are a beginner and put yourself in the chef's hands, he will introduce you gently, starting with some of the few cooked varieties of sushi. Eventually you will be seduced into trying a bite of raw tuna, and you'll be hooked. The next thing you know, you'll be sneaking into sushi bars alone so you won't have to share your eel, cruising the streets looking for undiscovered sushi bars, seeking out the chef with the most exotic selection and the freshest fish.

This book is a complete guide to sushi, its variety, its origins, and the customs, etiquette, and repertoire of the American sushi bar. It includes a guide to making sushi at home, a word on its nutritional benefits, a Japanese lesson, and a wealth of information that will help you order the obscure as well as the obvious the next time you're at a sushi bar. With sushi, as with any ethnic cuisine, if you don't have the inside information, you won't get the best it has to offer.

A passion for sushi invariably gives rise to curiosity about Japan, for clearly, such a glorious cuisine could only be the product of a remarkable culture. When you enter a sushi bar, you step into foreign territory. Its language, style, and hospitality are little affected by its American setting, and by sampling the food and getting involved in the theatricality of the sushi bar, you can cease to be an observer of Japanese culture and become instead a participant and an initiate.

This book, then, is not only an invitation to enjoy a delightful cuisine; it is also a passport to explore the unique culture that engendered it. *"Irasshaimase!"* the sushi chef will say as you walk into a sushi bar—welcome to the pleasures of sushi.

Japan is an island nation, its surrounding seas warmed by Kuroshio, the plankton-rich Japan Current, and abundant with an astonishing variety of fish and shellfish. The islands themselves are mountainous, and what little arable land exists is terraced and carefully cultivated to coax rice and a few other crops from the earth. Japan has always fed its dense population from the sea and the rice fields, its cuisine emphasizing what nature provides. Sushi, the combination of raw fish and seasoned rice that seems so exotic to us, is a supremely logical food in Japan.

Sushi began centuries ago in Japan as a method of preserving fish. Cleaned, raw fish were pressed between layers of salt and rice and weighted with a stone. After a few weeks, the stone was removed and replaced with a light cover, and a few months after that, the fermented fish and rice were considered ready to eat. Some restaurants in Tōkyō still serve this original style of sushi, called *narezushi,* made with freshwater carp. Its flavor is so strong that it obscures the fish's identity altogether, and narezushi is something of an acquired taste.

It wasn't until the eighteenth century that a clever chef named Yohei decided to forego the fermentation and serve sushi in something resembling its present form. It became very popular and two distinct styles emerged—Kansai style, from the city of Ōsaka in the Kansai region, and Edo style, from Tōkyō, which was then called Edo. Ōsaka has always been the commercial capital of Japan, and the rice merchants there developed sushi that consisted primarily of seasoned rice mixed with other ingredients and formed into decorative, edible packages. Tōkyō, located on a bay then rich with fish and shellfish, produced nigirizushi, featuring a select bit of seafood on a small pad of seasoned rice. Although the ornamental sushi of the Kansai region is still very popular, it is nigirizushi that is associated with the fine art of the sushi tradition.

This tradition owes a great deal to the affection that the Japanese have for nature. Nowhere is that affection more evident than in the kitchen. In Japanese cooking, the virtuosity of the chef is considered secondary to the quality and beauty of the ingredients themselves. It is a cuisine of presentation, not transformation, and much Japanese food is served uncooked, or nearly so, in small portions elegantly arranged to enhance its natural beauty. Sushi, breathtaking to look at as well as to eat, is a manifestation of these values.

# ORIGINS

The Japanese emphasis on the artful arrangement of food carries over into the way that sushi is served. Sushi is eaten in counter-style restaurants where highly skilled chefs make it to order and present it with panache. It can be made at home, but most Japanese prefer to leave sushi making to the experts. In a country where dining out amounts to a national pastime, there are more sushi bars than any other kind of restaurant. The style and personalized service of the sushi bar reflect what the Japanese expect when they dine out.

The Japanese do not entertain much at home—husbands and wives rarely socialize together, most houses are small, and only an immodest man would suggest that his home was fit to entertain an important guest. Instead, Japanese hospitality is extended in restaurants, which are, in a sense, the living rooms of Japan—retreats from the pressures of life and places to enjoy the company of friends.

In addition, much of the nation's business takes place in restaurants. Businessmen avoid dealing with strangers and will spend several evenings together before entering into any sort of negotiations. According to their thinking, a contract between strangers is little more than a piece of paper, but an agreement made with someone for whom you have poured sake is an agreement to be honored. The government considers this sort of entertaining so essential to the prosperity of Japan that its costs are totally tax deductible, amounting to a sizable subsidy of the restaurant business. The result is an extraordinary level of quality and personal service unknown and unaffordable in the United States.

Sushi is a product of Japan's tradition of service, its aesthetic, its cuisine. The conviviality and cordiality of the sushi bar, the elegant presentation of each order and its remarkable and unique taste have made sushi a passion in Japan and now in the United States as well. Deluged as we are in America with impersonal restaurants and microwave cooking, we crave genuine service and first-rate food. We have found both in the Japanese sushi tradition.

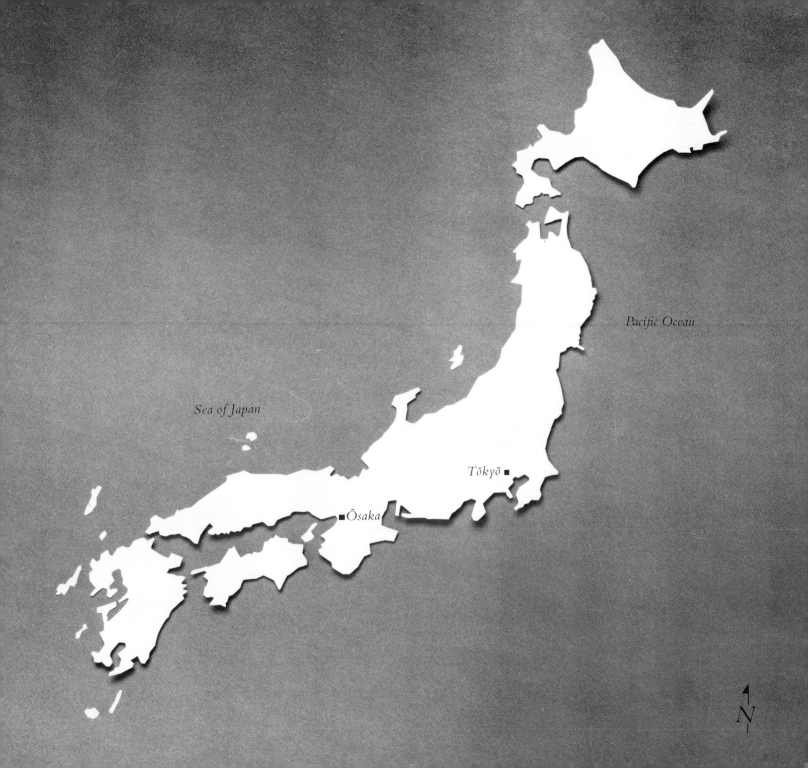

Sushi bars are intimate places. The extraordinary personal service offered there cannot be extended to many people at once, so sushi bars are usually small. If they are part of large Japanese restaurants, they are tucked into separate rooms where the smells of cooked food will not interfere with the delicate flavors of the fresh fish. Ten to twenty stools face a tiered, sloping counter, usually of polished light wood. Behind the counter, on a raised platform, the chef performs his feats of culinary legerdemain. Along the top of the counter, in an immaculately polished glass case, the day's catch is displayed—an array of fish, roe, and shellfish on a bed of crushed ice.

Usually, stand-up menus are placed on the bar, with pictures of various sushi and their names in Japanese and English. In bars frequented mainly by Japanese customers, there may be no picture menus. Instead, a large wooden plaque on the wall lists the offerings in Japanese characters, and you may have to point to get what you want.

In many sushi bars, you will have to wait for a seat at the counter. Few accept reservations, because it's hard to predict how long a customer will stay. Some people pop in for a quick snack and a beer. Others linger for hours over conversation and round after round of sushi, so order a sake and relax while you wait. There may be a few tables available where you can order a platter of sushi or sashimi, although you will miss the theatrics of the chef and the lively exchange with other customers.

When choosing a sushi bar, look for cleanliness above all else. Compromises in housekeeping are omens of things to come. The best sushi bars have a sense of visual order and dignity, though the atmosphere may be quite festive. The fish on display in the sushi case should have the vibrant look of freshness, and cooked meals should not be served at the bar or in the same room. And, of course, the presence of a Japanese clientele indicates that the chef's standards please their more experienced taste buds.

Sushi prices vary from bar to bar and from item to item, but you can expect to pay from two to three dollars an order (two pieces) for nigirizushi. Rolled sushi costs a little less, but goes a lot further toward filling an empty stomach. Sashimi may be as expensive as several orders of sushi, but ordered first and lingered over, it will satisfy a craving for protein and an appetite for beauty. Most people can easily eat a dozen pieces of sushi, and with sake, the bill can reach twenty dollars for one person.

The seemingly casual way that prices and bills are handled in sushi bars can make Americans used to price tags and printed menus uneasy. Rest assured that discretion, not exploitation, is at work, and if you are on a limited budget you might want to tell your chef what it is ahead of time, so you can relax.

# THE SUSHI BAR

There is a formality in all Japanese restaurants that tends to fluster even the most mannerly Americans. Sushi bars are no exception. Although the extraordinary hospitality of the Japanese prevents them from snubbing you for a breach of manners, you may enjoy your meal more if you know something about sushi-bar etiquette.

As you are seated, a waitress will bring you a hot towel, *oshibori,* wrapped in cellophane or rolled up on a basket tray. It is an invitation to wipe your hands. Fold it and put it back on the counter or in the basket when you've finished. Many restaurants leave it for you to use during the meal, but a regular napkin will also be provided for your lap.

Each place at the bar is marked by a small saucer, a pair of *hashi,* Japanese chopsticks, and sometimes, *hashi oki,* a ceramic holder for chopsticks. Hashi are wrapped in paper and joined at the top to show they have never been used. Unwrap them, separate them, and lean them against the hashi oki, if it is provided, or against the edge of your saucer. When they are not in your hand, chopsticks belong directly in front of you, parallel with the edge of the counter. Many people rub their chopsticks together to sand off splinters, but a good sushi bar uses high-quality hashi, and it is considered bad manners not to notice the difference. Besides, you might start a fire.

The waitress will ask if you want something to drink. Sake, tea, or beer is appropriate, and you may wish to order a bowl of soup from her—*suimono,* which is clear broth, or *misoshiru,* made with fermented soybean paste. Everything else, which should be strictly sashimi or sushi, you should order from the chef standing in front of you. It is impolite to ask him for drinks or other kinds of food.

If you do order soup, it will be served in a covered bowl to keep it piping hot—optimum temperature by Japanese standards. You may find it too hot, but in Japan, slurping, which cools soup off a bit, is perfectly proper. So uncover the bowl, hold it in one hand, pick out the tidbits in it with your chopsticks, and drink the broth like tea, slurping if you dare—after all, your mom will never know.

# E T I Q U E T T E

Experienced sushi buffs often start each meal with an order of assorted sashimi, to give the chef an opportunity to show off the best of the day's selection. Sashimi is arranged on a plate that the chef places on the slanted part of the bar. You may leave it there or bring it down to the counter in front of you, but in either case, pick up each piece of sashimi separately with your chopsticks—it is not finger food.

Shredded *daikon,* a large, mild white radish, and *wasabi,* a pale green, fiery variety of horseradish, always accompany sashimi. The daikon serves as a palate refresher and is eaten with chopsticks. The wasabi is meant to be mixed with soy sauce, in the saucer at your place, to create a dipping sauce for the sashimi. Don't make wasabi soup. Most Americans overseason Japanese food, and sushi chefs are horrified to see their delicate fish drowned in sauce. Dip an edge of sashimi into the saucer and pop the whole piece into your mouth. Japanese food is served in bite-sized morsels, and sashimi is so tender it dissolves in your mouth without the struggle you would expect with a similar portion of rare roast beef.

When you are ready for sushi, the chef will place a square plate or wooden tray on the slanted part of the bar where both he and you can reach it. Then he will put each order on the plate, or he may simply serve the sushi right on the countertop. Either way, he'll set out a mound of thinly sliced pickled ginger, *gari,* for you to nibble on between sushi courses.

Order your sushi by the name of the fish served on top—you can use the stand-up plastic menu on the counter as a guide or you can point at things in the case, but it is customary and most enjoyable to order one or two things at a time, according to your whim and the chef's suggestions. Spontaneity and the interplay between customer and chef are a major part of the appeal of eating sushi.

Sushi is always served in pairs. The Japanese avoid serving anything sliced in ones or threes, since the words for "one slice," *hito kire,* are a pun for the words "to kill a man," and *mi kire,* "three slices," is a pun on the phrase "to kill myself." If you ask for an order of sushi, you'll get two pieces. If you ask for two of anything, you'll get two orders. The exception is rolled sushi—one order means one roll cut into several pieces.

Sushi is finger food. It is designed to be picked up, dipped in soy sauce, and then eaten in one or two bites. Chopsticks are acceptable, but since sushi is served across the counter from you, you will be taking unnecessary risks trying to maneuver it from counter to sauce to mouth with hashi. As one chef demurely explained, you might drop it in your dish of soy sauce and splash on your companion—most impolite.

There is a proper technique for getting sushi off the counter and into your mouth. Pick it up by the far end, so you can flip it over, and dip the fish side, *not* the rice, briefly into the soy sauce, then put it into your mouth so the fish lands on your taste buds. Sushi chefs wince at the American habit of soaking the rice in soy sauce till it's black. The delicate seasonings of the rice are obscured and the rice pad disintegrates on the spot, or directly over your lap. Dipping the rice in soy sauce, one chef explained, is like pouring ketchup all over the outside of your hamburger bun.

It is customary in sushi bars to offer your chef a beer or sake, although this is not expected. If he accepts, order it from the waitress. His sake is likely to be served in a mug, which he will raise in a toast to thank you. *Kanpai* means "to your health."

You should avoid smoking at a sushi bar for the same reason that cooked meals are not served there. The conflicting odors all but obliterate the delicate flavors of the fish for the people around you.

You may linger at the sushi bar as long as you wish, although it is decent to consider the growing desperation of the people waiting for your seat. When you are finished, ask the waitress, not the chef, for a check, *okanjō*. The chef will tally up the bill and give it to the waitress, who will present it to you and take your money. In Japanese restaurants, people who handle food never handle money. The culture as a whole considers money vulgar and tries to make as little of it as possible. In Japan, the gratuity is included in the bill. The Japanese take pride in excellent service and do not like to feel they have to be bribed to do a good job. You are in the United States, however, and a substantial tip should be left at your place—consider the quality of personal service you have enjoyed and the fact that the tip will be shared by the chefs, the kitchen helpers, and the waitresses.

Etiquette is so important in Japan and table manners so elaborate that Americans are not expected to have any at all, and almost anything you do will be excused. These details may interest you, however, if you are considering joining the foreign service or enjoy reflecting on the cultural implications of such details:

Avoid picking up a piece of food, biting off half, and putting the remainder back on your plate.

You may pick your teeth at the table, but the Japanese do so with the free hand demurely covering the mouth like a fan.

Do not pass food from one person to another with chopsticks. This parallels the Japanese funeral ceremony of passing the cremated bones of a deceased relative between family members.

If you help yourself from a communal plate, use the back ends of your chopsticks.

Do your best not to leave food on your plate. Japan is a country that is used to scarcity, and wasting food is a serious transgression there. Also, the Japanese are repulsed by the idea of leaving garbage at the table. In days past, noblemen were so loath to leave unsightly things behind that they wrapped fish bones and fruit pits in paper carried for this purpose, and tucked the little packages into the sleeves of their kimonos. This is not expected in a sushi bar. If you don't like sea urchin roe, you don't have to put it in your pocket, but do try to clean your plate.

According to Japanese thinking, the best way to cook a fish is not to. Sashimi is fresh, raw seafood served chilled and sliced and elegantly arranged. It is the food most loved in Japan and the traditional prelude to sushi. Although many Americans are reluctant to eat anything more wiggly than a carrot without cooking it first, a single bite of succulent, subtle sashimi is usually adequate persuasion.

Sashimi should be prepared from fish fresh from the water, iced but preferably not frozen, as the thawing process can leach out subtle flavors. The fish should be taken from the purest waters, and though a wide variety of fish and shellfish can be made into sashimi, freshwater fish are rarely served because of the possibility of parasites.

For the sushi bar, the head chef selects the day's fish himself and will accept nothing less than the best from his suppliers. He considers when a specimen is at the peak of its season and when and where it was caught. He looks for firm, fragrant flesh, bright red, healthy gills, and clear eyes, or, in the case of shellfish, a tightly closed shell.

Although the ideal is immaculate freshness, many fish freeze respectably, and chefs may prefer frozen fish flown in from Japan over the local catch. Many fish traditionally served in sushi bars are found only in Japanese waters and must be imported. More important, fish caught by our fishing fleet are often handled carelessly, and by the time they reach market, they may be too old or too bruised to be served as sushi. The Japanese, on the other hand, are more respectful of their catch, and a properly handled frozen specimen may be superior to a damaged but fresh local fish. When a chef chooses to serve frozen fish or shellfish, you can be sure that it is the best available and that it meets his high standards.

Since slicing the fish is the equivalent of cooking it, sashimi slicing techniques have evolved into a formalized art. Fish cut thick or thin make an entirely different impression on the taste buds, and the precise technique for slicing a particular fish is a matter of longstanding tradition.

# S A S H I M I

- *Hira zukuri* [top left] is a rectangular cut, three-eighths inch thick and the size of a domino. It can be used for almost any fish, particularly those with fragile flesh that might get mushy if handled too much.

- *Ito zukuri* [top right] is the thread cut, for fish with very thin fillets such as squid. The strips are cut about two inches long and a sixteenth of an inch thick and arranged in a haystack or chrysanthemum shape.

- *Kaku zukuri* [bottom right] is the cube cut, and it is used for fish, such as tuna and yellowtail, with thick, soft flesh. The cubes are three-quarters of an inch in all dimensions.

- *Usu zukuri* [bottom left] is a paper-thin slice, so thin the pattern on a piece of china can be seen through the sashimi. This cut is used for firm, white-fleshed fish such as sea bass and halibut. The slices are less than a sixteenth of an inch thick and are often arranged in decorative patterns.

Thick sashimi is usually served with regular soy sauce, thinner cuts with delicate *ponzu,* a tangy, citrus-flavored soy sauce. Various spices such as wasabi, red pepper, and sliced green onion may be served to mix with the sauces, and sashimi is always served on a cloud of curly, shredded daikon. Sometimes green or purple seaweed, cucumber, or other taste refreshers, called *tsuma,* are also on the plate. Thinly sliced lemon may be interspersed between slices of certain fish to tighten the flesh and cut through oiliness.

Sashimi is fish presented in its simplest and most beautiful form. Lay a bite-sized piece of this art work on a pad of sushi rice and you have nigirizushi.

The Japanese word for rice, *gohan,* translates as "honorable food." Rice is eaten with every meal, and the Japanese are so obsessed with it that every available corner of land is cultivated, even though such surpluses have built up that storage is a national problem.

It is difficult for Americans to appreciate the reverence the Japanese feel for rice. For centuries it was the standard of wealth, the measure of a man's fortune. Even after a cash economy developed, samurai warriors still took their pay in rice (which they ingeniously cooked in the field by tying up the grains in a cloth, soaking it in a stream, then burying the parcel and building a fire over it). Rice is *the* national delicacy, and it's judged for quality and texture with the same discerning affection the French bring to wine. It is unthinkable to leave rice in your bowl. A man may be forgiven for squandering money, but he will be condemned for wasting rice.

The skillful preparation of a good batch of rice is the measure of every Japanese cook. Precise timing and control of heat is essential, and gas or electric rice cookers, which guarantee perfect results, have become standard equipment in most kitchens. Short-grained rice is used exclusively. Tender and moist, it is clingy enough to be eaten with chopsticks.

Rice is the foundation of sushi. It is prepared a special way and called *shari*. Every chef has his own recipe, but sushi rice is always steamed and then tossed in a dressing made of rice vinegar, sugar, and salt while an assistant stands by fanning the rice to cool it quickly, giving it the chewiness and glossy sheen prized by sushi connoisseurs. It takes years of practice to prepare shari properly, and years more to master the technique of forming it into pads of the right size and consistency for nigirizushi.

Every year, in the heart of Tōkyō, the emperor of Japan plants and tends a tiny rice field in the imperial gardens as a ritual of respect for this simple food, the very basis of Japan's health and survival.

# R I C E

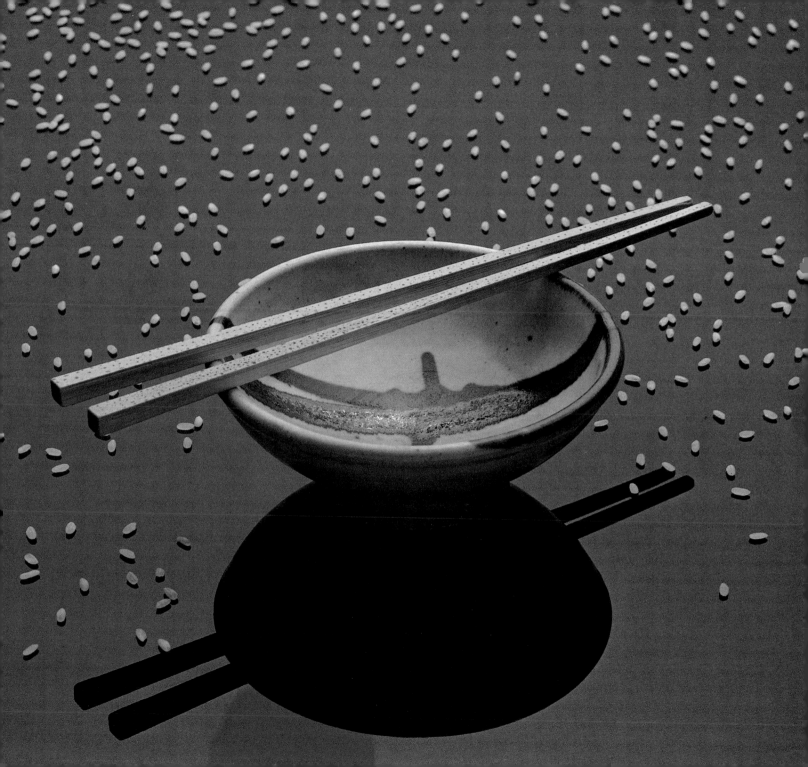

Nigirizushi is possibly the most artful branch of Japanese cuisine, and it is certainly the supreme product of the sushi tradition. *Nigiri* means "pressed in the hand," and the chef forms a small oval of sushi rice in one hand, then presses a choice strip of fish or shellfish on top. Fish roe is also served as nigirizushi, on a pad of rice wrapped with a band of seaweed deep enough to contain the rice and hold the roe on top. This style of nigirizushi is called *gunkan,* which means "boat," and is also used to serve tiny shellfish and other small ingredients that might otherwise go their own way.

Most varieties of nigirizushi contain a hint of pungent wasabi horseradish, and are meant to be dipped in soy sauce. Some seafood in nigirizushi is cooked, but these are exceptions. Fresh raw fish, shellfish, and roe are the prime ingredients in nigirizushi.

Fish is the largest category on the sushi-bar menu. The same care that goes into the selection and preparation of fish for sashimi applies to nigirizushi as well. Only the best specimens and the choicest cuts are used, and whether the fish is an exotic import or a fresh-out-of-the-water local, the chef's expertise assures you that the quality will be high.

The splendid array of shellfish used for nigirizushi can be almost bewildering to most Americans, who may have little more than a passing familiarity with clam chowder and shrimp cocktail. Most of the menu items are exotic varieties imported from Japan, but local shellfish will turn up occasionally, as well as rare delicacies not on the menu. With shellfish in particular, you will do well to explore the selection with the chef.

Several kinds of fish roe are served in sushi bars, most of them processed and imported from Japan. A few are available fresh on occasion and are gently marinated in sake and soy sauce, giving them a less salty flavor than the processed kinds. The tingling flavors and intriguing textures of roe are only surpassed by their beauty; the gemlike reds, oranges, and golds seem to glow in the sushi case.

What follows is an illustrated and annotated sushi menu. You will find descriptions of the standard items served in most American sushi bars, plus many not-so-standard ones, with their Japanese names and English equivalents. Japanese is the predominant language in sushi bars in America, and fish are called by Japanese names even when the actual species served may be a distant American cousin. Sushi chefs are concerned with quality and flavor, not ichthyology. The nomenclature may be approximate, but the standards will be firm.

# NIGIRIZUSHI

*Maguro*

*Toro*

- *Maguro* (tuna). Tuna is the fish most Americans associate with sashimi and sushi—more of it is sold in sushi bars than any other kind of fish. Raw tuna has a soft, meaty texture and clean taste that win over many sushi skeptics at first bite.

  In Japan, tuna is greatly prized as a food fish. What little tuna is eaten in America is canned, and at first it may be difficult for you to believe that the flavorful deep-red flesh of *maguro* is any relation at all to the chunky main ingredient of school-lunch sandwiches or Friday-night casseroles.

  There are many varieties of tuna, but the kind you'll most likely encounter in an American sushi bar is a relatively lean cut of bluefin or yellowfin tuna, both of which are available year round, fresh from American waters. Tuna also freezes well, so there is always maguro in the sushi case. However, as is true for all fish, tuna's quality varies from season to season. Prime specimens are generally caught in the winter, from November to February. Despite its availability and consistent good taste, in the spring and summer tuna may be inferior to less familiar fish that are at their peak. Sample maguro at different times of the year and, as always, seek the sushi chef's recommendation.

- *Toro* (fatty tuna belly). In Japan, tuna are graded and priced according to fat content—the fattiest part of the fish is the most prized—and *toro,* cut from the tuna's belly, is usually the most expensive item on a sushi menu. Toro is pink and somewhat opaque, and the sushi chef may identify it as *chūtoro,* which is moderately fat, or *ōtoro,* which indicates the highest fat content, tuna that is light pink and extraordinarily tender.

  Toro is taken only from bluefin tuna, which are abundant in the waters off the East Coast. Bluefin have never been commercially important in the United States except as pet food, partly because the fish are so enormous that they are awkward for fishermen to handle. Many specimens caught are the size of a baby elephant, and when the cat-food market is down, they are often thrown back. The same fish flown to Japan could command an exorbitant price.

  A taste of toro goes a long way toward explaining why. Its richness and tenderness approach that of butter. In the winter, when toro, like maguro, is at its best, it is a luxurious and tasty delicacy well worth its price. Out of season, however, it may not live up to its reputation or its price tag.

Shiro maguro

Hamachi

- *Shiro maguro* (albacore). Albacore is the source of top-grade canned tuna in the United States, where its delicacy and excellent flavor can scarcely be discerned midst the mayonnaise. Its Japanese name means "white tuna," and albacore flesh ranges from rose to pale peach in color. Its flavor is rich but not overbearing.

  Albacore meat is so soft that it is difficult to handle. It also changes color quickly in the sushi case, although this does not indicate deterioration. For these reasons, many sushi chefs choose not to serve it. Even when it is available, *shiro maguro* is almost never on a sushi-bar menu—one more reason to ask your chef, *"Kyō wa nani ga oishii desu ka?"*—"What's good today?"

  The albacore is abundant in Pacific waters, uncommon in the Atlantic, and in season July through October in the United States. If you have the good fortune to come across shiro maguro, don't miss the opportunity to try it as sushi or sashimi.

- *Hamachi* (young yellowtail). Yellowtail is the common name of a number of species of amberjack—sleek migratory fish similar to the tunas. The Japanese variety called *hamachi* has light golden flesh and may display a dark streak along the edge of a fillet, a characteristic of the two-toned musculature of fish that cruise the open seas. Since hamachi is not listed on many American sushi menus, it may be overlooked. It's one of the most rewarding discoveries you can make at a sushi bar.

  Hamachi can be as rich as toro, smooth and buttery with a deep smoky taste, but not as overpoweringly fatty. The area around the pectoral fins is considered the tastiest part and is often set aside for special customers. Some sushi bars grill the skeleton and the bits of meat left on it and serve it as an appetizer or snack.

  Although varieties of yellowtail are plentiful in waters off both U.S. coasts, hamachi are usually flown in frozen from Japan, where they are raised in hatcheries and harvested when they weigh between fifteen and twenty pounds—just right for sushi. Yellowtail caught here are usually too lean to qualify.

  Hamachi is available for import year round, but you may have to try a few sushi bars before you find it.

*Katsuo*          *Kohada*

■ *Katsuo* (bonito). The bonito, also called the skipjack tuna, is a small migratory fish that is common in the warm waters of the Pacific. Its meat is a deep rosy color and is prized for its rich flavor. Bonito does not freeze well, and it is best eaten only in season and only where it can be caught locally. Look for *katsuo* in West Coast sushi bars from midsummer to early fall.

The migration of bonito to Japanese waters marks the beginning of spring. The Japanese are very sentimental about the change of seasons, and they treasure the first mushroom, the first blossom, the first fish of each one. Though the early arrivals are not as tasty as the katsuo caught later in the season, they are valued even more. Sodo, a seventeenth century poet, wrote this haiku celebrating the harbingers of spring:

> *Behold the green leaves!*
> *A thrush singing in the hills—*
> *The first bonito.*

■ *Kohada* (Japanese shad). *Kohada* is called "young punctatus" on standard sushi-bar menus—but "punctatus" is really just the second half of its species name, and kohada has no exact North American equivalent. Suffice it to say that the fish is a shad and a member of the herring family. It is about four inches long with silvery gray skin decorated with a fancy pattern of black dots. Similar fish are caught along the East Coast and may be substituted for kohada, but most sushi bars import the genuine item frozen from Japan.

Kohada have strongly flavored white flesh that the sushi chef marinates in vinegar. Usually, he slices or crosshatches the skin, and some chefs with a flair for the decorative may even braid the kohada over the sushi rice.

Perhaps because of its strong flavor, kohada is uncommon except in sushi bars that cater primarily to a Japanese clientele. The fainthearted may find it a bit overpowering, but if you like herring, you'll probably like kohada. When you come across it in the sushi case, give it a try—even if you aren't crazy about the taste, you're sure to love the way it looks.

*Saba*

■ *Saba* (mackerel). The mackerel is a rich, oily fish with soft but substantial flesh. Prime specimens are caught in October and November. Young mackerel are very sensitive to environmental changes, and you may find mackerel fabulously plentiful one year, scarce the next.

The mackerel and the tuna are members of the same family, but the two have little in common from the point of view of flavor. Tuna has a light, subtle taste; mackerel's taste is somewhat more insistent. Both fish have a two-toned musculature, with distinct bands of light and dark flesh, and when you order *saba* in a sushi bar, you will see these two kinds of muscles in a single biteful.

The sushi chef lightly salts and marinates saba for a few days. By the time it makes it to the sushi case, it is very tender, and its distinctive taste will vary with each chef's marinade. Saba is not only used in nigirizushi. It is the fish ingredient in various Kansai-style sushi that are layered with rice and seaweed, with the emphasis on rice.

Several kinds of mackerel are available in the United States and in Japan, but most saba served in American sushi bars is flown in frozen from Japan. Mackerel must be put on ice within six hours of being caught or their flavor is lost, and Japanese fishermen go to great lengths to protect mackerel's quality. The best mackerel is caught at its peak during a few weeks in the heart of winter, frozen and used throughout the year.

Saba is extremely flavorful, but it is a bit much for some people. If you like strong-tasting fish, try saba at your first opportunity. It is likely to become one of your favorites.

*Sake*

■ *Sake* (salmon). Salmon is perhaps the most easily recognized fish in the sushi case, its bright orange color almost too vibrant to be real. Its taste is equally remarkable, and salmon is treasured as a food fish by all cultures blessed with its migrations. In recent decades, the Atlantic salmon has been nearly wiped out by pollution and is now rare in Europe as well. Only Pacific salmon are still plentiful, and in most sushi bars, varieties from Japan and Alaska are used.

Salmon grow fat and robust in the ocean, then head for fresh water where they swim upstream to spawn. During this heroic journey they do not eat, and they deteriorate rapidly. Only those caught at sea are considered suitable for sushi. Salmon is never served raw in sushi bars; it is lightly smoked or cured for a few days in salt and sugar. It tastes sweet, sometimes smoky, and is always meltingly tender. Occasionally, fresh grilled salmon is served as nigirizushi. Its color is pale peach; its flavor more delicate than uncooked salmon.

In Japanese, the words for rice wine and salmon are spelled identically and pronounced very much the same, leading some people to worry that they may be ordering a bottle of fish by mistake. The word for the beverage is pronounced sah-kay. For the fish, the last syllable is slightly clipped, sah-keh, with an *e* as in *led*. If this is too fine a distinction, you can order the fish as sha-kay, as it is pronounced in northern Japan. You will also avoid confusion by ordering your fish from the sushi chef and your beverages from the waitress, as is proper.

Tai

Hirame

Suzuki

- *Tai* (porgy, red snapper). Although *tai,* translated as "sea bream," appears on standard sushi menus, the fish the Japanese call tai is not available in the United States. Instead, porgy and red snapper fill in for tai in American sushi bars. Porgy is a close relation to tai, but red snapper is related to the Japanese fish in taste only. Both are sweet, lean fish with broad-flaked pink-and-white flesh.

  Although the American versions may make excellent sushi, they do not have the character or flavor uncooked that make tai a Japanese favorite. When you try tai, ask the chef exactly what it is he's serving. In another season or on another coast, you may be served a different fish altogether.

- *Hirame* (halibut). Halibut are odd, flat fish that flutter across the ocean floor like swimming crepes. A halibut begins life swimming upright like a typical fish. Eventually, however, it begins listing to one side, and as it gets closer to the horizontal, its bottom eye doesn't get much of a view and moves around next to its top eye, giving it a slightly alarming, Cubist sort of visage.

  No matter. Beneath this homely exterior is pale pink translucent flesh, a delicate flavor, and the makings of an excellent sushi. Halibut also make superior sashimi. Cut into paper-thin transparent slices, it is called *hirame usu zukuri,* and it may be served with the slices in the center arranged like a flower, a flourish called *hana zukuri.*

  Halibut is available fresh year round from American waters, but it is at its best in December and January.

- *Suzuki* (sea bass). *Suzuki* is a Japanese fish without an exact equivalent in America. Various fish that fall into the sea bass category are served as suzuki here. Sea bass have shiny white flesh with an easily recognizable broad-flaked structure and a mild flavor. The sea bass season in U.S. waters is limited to the summer months, and many sushi bars offer it only then, when it is available fresh. You may also encounter it flown in frozen from Japan.

  Like hirame, suzuki makes an elegant paper-thin sashimi, *suzuki usu zukuri,* which is as pleasant to pronounce as it is to eat. Suzuki sashimi is often served with ponzu, a lemony soy sauce, or served in the summertime on a bed of ice cubes with tangy *shiso* leaf and a scattering of red pepper flakes.

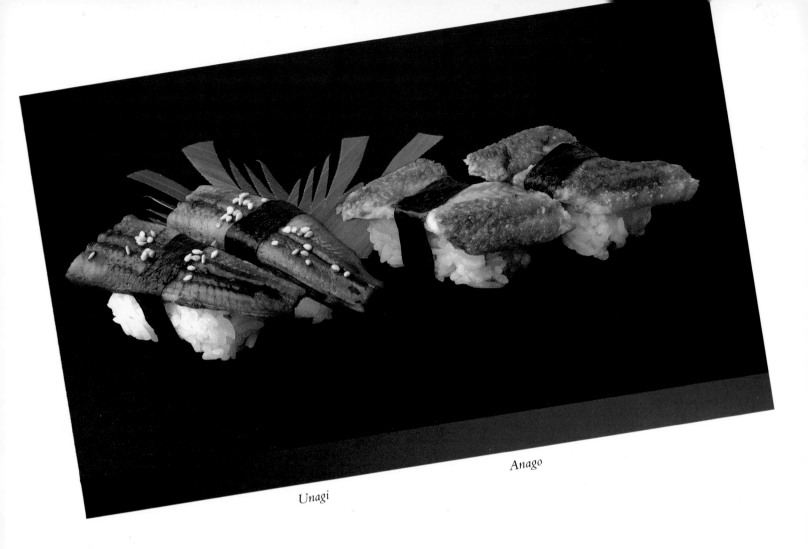

Unagi

Anago

- *Unagi* (freshwater eel). Every year during the summer solstice, on the Day of the Cow, everyone in Japan eats eel. It is believed that if you eat eel on Cow Day, you will be healthy all year, and the Japanese are so faithful to the tradition that some 865 tons of *unagi* are consumed in a twenty-four-hour period.

  Cow Day unagi is usually cut into small pieces, dipped in a sauce, skewered, and cooked over charcoal. Surprisingly, it is prepared in much the same way for sushi—unagi is never served raw. Instead, it is precooked—grilled—and lightly grilled again on a hibachi at the bar. It is glazed with *tare,* a sweet, smoky sauce made by simmering eel broth, sugar, and soy sauce for two days.

  Though there is an equally tasty American species of freshwater eel, sushi chefs prefer to import prepared unagi from Japan, where eels are carefully cultivated in hatcheries in lakes and lagoons and are precooked before they are exported.

  Unagi is almost always available in sushi bars. It has a rich taste and a nut-brown color, and because it is served already seasoned with tare, it should not be dipped in soy sauce. Unagi makes an excellent first step for the beginning sushi eater, and it is particularly good combined with cucumber in a rolled sushi.

- *Anago* (marine eel). *Anago* is served in the same style as unagi in sushi bars. It is precooked, grilled at the bar, and basted in tare. Anago is initially boiled, however, not grilled.

  Both unagi and anago are important sources of animal fat in the Japanese diet, but anago is the leaner of the two, and its golden flesh is therefore not quite as rich as unagi's and not quite as popular with the Japanese.

  Though there are similar species available fresh from American waters, the Japanese variety is considered superior and anago is imported precooked from Japan. It is available year round in American sushi bars. Like unagi, anago is sometimes combined with cucumber in a rolled sushi.

*Tako*　　　　　　　　*Ika*

- *Tako* (octopus). The burgundy tentacles of the octopus are the most easily identified delicacy in the sushi case. Despite its scary reputation, the octopus is a timid creature that weighs just a few pounds. Octopuses feed on crab, lobster, abalone, clams, and scallops, and with such a gourmet diet it is no surprise that their flesh is rich in protein and flavor. The octopus is common in the Pacific Ocean, and although much of the world's catch is from the California coast, the *tako* in most sushi cases is a variety from Japan that looks prettier sliced. It is imported frozen and is available year round.

  Tako is always boiled, which tenderizes the flesh and causes the limp gray tentacles to curl, become firm, and turn a deep rose color. The tentacles are sliced very thin for sushi, revealing white flesh under the wine-colored skin. Tako offers the slightest resistance to the bite and has a clean, subtle taste that will appeal to all shellfish lovers.

- *Ika* (squid). This exotic member of the shellfish family has no outer shell and swims freely in the ocean, its long tentacles trailing behind it. Squid species range from inch-long miniatures to the sixty-foot giant that scared the daylights out of Captain Nemo in *Twenty Thousand Leagues under the Sea*. Over eighty percent of the creature is edible, and squid is a plentiful and largely unexploited food source.

  Squid flesh is pearly white and glossy, and when rolled up in the sushi case it looks more like pasta than fish. Although the tentacles, called *geso,* can be ordered grilled, it is the firm, flat flesh of the body that is ordinarily served. *Ika* is sliced and scored slightly to tenderize it and give the soy sauce something to cling to. It is always brought in frozen from Japan; *mongō ika,* a Japanese species, is the variety most often served in sushi bars. It has a resilient, almost sticky texture, and the iodiney sea taste will send you into rapture or leave you cold. In some sushi bars the chefs serve it grilled, sprinkled with lemon juice and salt, or tare, the sweet dark sauce served on eel. Imported frozen squid is available year round.

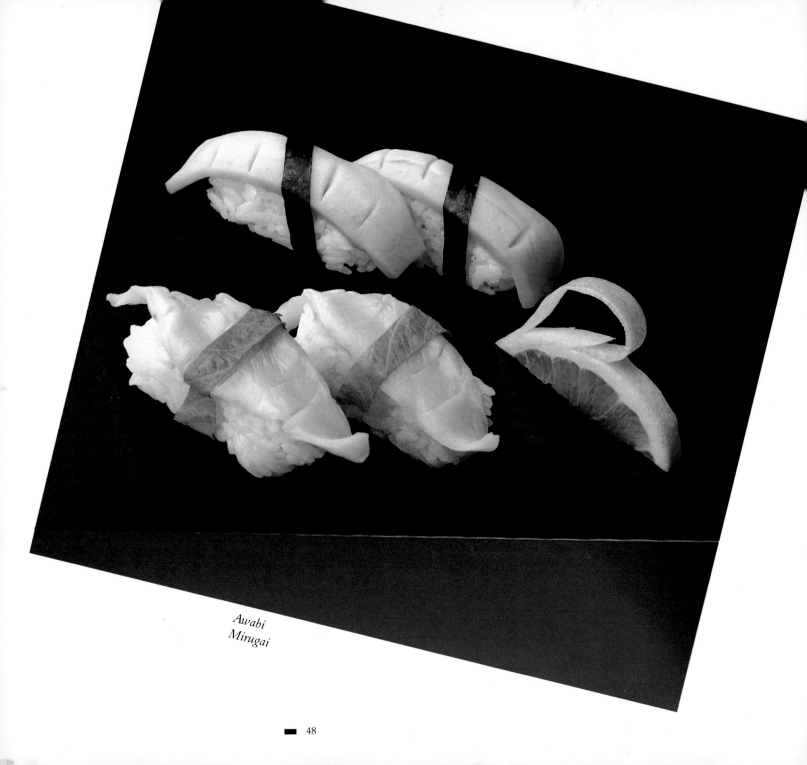

*Awabi*
*Mirugai*

- *Awabi* (abalone). The abalone is a sea snail. Called a sea ear because of its shape, abalone is prized for its mother-of-pearl inner shell and the subtle, unique flavor of its edible "foot." In Japan, *awabi* are cultivated commercially and over 16,000 metric tons are taken each year. But most American sushi bars get their abalone from the much smaller numbers taken along the U.S. Pacific coast, where there are eight abalone species to choose from.

  In the sushi case, abalone is displayed in a shell, although not necessarily the one it arrived in. The meat of a market-sized abalone is about an inch thick and the size of a hand. Its color ranges from pale peach to gray. Japanese varieties are much smaller, and they may be gray or even blue.

  Abalone toughens as it cooks, so sushi is its most perfect manifestation. Even so, raw awabi is rubbery. For sushi, it is sliced across the grain and scored slightly to tenderize it and give the soy sauce something to stick to.

- *Mirugai* (geoduck). *Mirugai* is a large hardshell clam most often called geoduck (pronounced goo-ey-duck) or horseneck clam in America. It is extremely popular on the West Coast where it is plentiful and always fresh. A geoduck, with its thick "neck" or siphon, can be well over a foot long. The siphon never retracts into the rather too small shell, and a geoduck presents an alarming visage in the sushi case, resembling as it does a part of the human male anatomy.

  To assure himself and the customer of its freshness, the sushi chef ceremoniously gives a geoduck a good whack on the counter, then watches it curl slightly before slicing it. An out-of-the-water geoduck stays vital for several days, although the chefs say it is not really alive. Ask the clam.

  Mirugai has a faint shellfish flavor and a pale peach color. It is slightly elastic to the bite. It is sliced thin for sushi or sashimi and often fringed on the edges for tenderness and decorative appeal.

Torigai        Aoyagi        Akagai

- *Torigai* (Japanese cockle). This small shellfish, imported from Japan, has black-and-white striped flesh. It is sliced very thin and makes a pretty sushi, but it is not available here fresh, and frozen *torigai* is rubbery. It is commonly served and quite popular, but you may be so busy swallowing it that you forget to notice the flavor.

- *Aoyagi* (Japanese red clam). This small clam is similar to our East Coast quahog (pronounced ko-hog), and it is imported frozen from Japan. Before it is served, *aoyagi* is plunged into boiling water to bring out the meat's bright orange color and make it firm. Then it is sliced very thin for sushi. Aoyagi is leafy tasting and delicious, and it is quite beautiful to look at.

- *Akagai* (pepitona clam). *Akagai* appears on many sushi menus, but this clam is hard to come by and rarely available. It is a variety imported frozen from Japan that is actually harvested in Korea or the Philippines. Its flesh is sweet and delicate, with a beautiful peach-to-orange color. Akagai is sliced thin and butterflied for sushi, and sometimes deep scoring makes it appear ribbed. Its threadlike edges, called *himo,* are considered a delicacy and are often served in rolled sushi with cucumber.

*Kobashira*          *Kaibashira*

- *Kobashira* (small scallops). In America, a scallop is the succulent muscle that opens and closes the shell of a particular shellfish, the one pictured above gas stations. The Japanese, however, refer to this muscle in all clams as a scallop, and the ones served as sushi usually come from aoyagi. They are a pale golden color, and they have a sweet shellfish taste. Because they are so small, they are served gunkan style. Though rarely on the menu, *kobashira* are often available in American sushi bars, and you may see them heaped in a glass dish in the sushi case.

- *Kaibashira* (large scallops). *Kaibashira* are giant clam adductor muscles. They are sliced for sushi, and the most common variety comes from a huge Japanese clam called *tairagai.* In the sushi case, kaibashira have a preposterous resemblance to marshmallows.

Kani          Ebi          Ama ebi

- *Kani* (crab). Crab is served cooked for sushi, and although varieties are available off both coasts in the Lower Forty-eight, most crab served in sushi bars is frozen king crab imported from Alaska. These long-legged, gangly creatures may weigh up to twenty pounds and produce succulent, firm chunks of coral-streaked white meat that are tidy to serve in sushi, but lose much of their flavor in the freezing process. They are caught in ice-cold rough waters off the Alaskan coast, and most ships process the catch on board and ship it out already cooked and frozen.

  Frozen crab, although pretty, meaty, and reassuringly familiar, is rather ordinary and may not be worth eating in a sushi bar, unless you aren't ready for raw fish. A popular West Coast aberration, the "California Special," is a rolled sushi made of cooked crab meat, avocado, and mayonnaise rolled in rice and seaweed. It is a tasty and harmless way to introduce someone to sushi, but it is as authentically Japanese as a peanut-butter-and-jelly sandwich.

- *Ebi* (cooked prawn). *Ebi* is one of the most popular items on the sushi menu. It is actually jumbo shrimp (a prawn is really a freshwater crustacean, but jumbo shrimp are called prawns in restaurants), and those served in American sushi bars are flown in frozen from Mexico. They are dropped in boiling salted water, then cleaned and split into a butterfly shape. Their firm, striped, pink-and-white flesh is a familiar treat for the sushi beginner timid about eating raw fish.

- *Ama ebi* (raw prawn). The Japanese consider fresh raw prawn one of the greatest delicacies in the sushi case. A cleaned, uncooked jumbo shrimp is glossy, almost transparent, and sweet. Fresh and frozen prawns are widely available—many varieties are caught on both coasts, but *ama ebi* is still a rare treat. Few prawns, fresh or frozen, are of a high enough quality to be served raw.

  In Japan, raw shrimp gourmandising is taken a step beyond ama ebi. *Odori*, "dancing prawns," so named because they dance around just before they are eaten (who wouldn't?), are said to tickle the palate when served raw, pulsating with not-quite-extinguished life. The Japanese pay as much as twenty dollars for this rare pleasure.

Ikura

Uni

- *Ikura* (salmon roe). *Ikura* is the most common roe in sushi bars and the one most familiar to American customers, because it is sometimes served as red caviar in our own cuisine. The large, glossy red-orange eggs—which are about the size of peas—are sticky and delicious. They look like Day-Glo bubble bath in their seaweed container, and ikura is one sushi that should not be turned upside down on its way to your mouth.

- *Uni* (sea urchin roe). A sea urchin is a shellfish that looks like a porcupine's back—not very appetizing. But sea urchin roe—actually the gonads—are considered a delicacy in many parts of the world. The globelike shell is divested of its spines for easy handling, then opened on the bottom. The insides are shaken out, and what's left, attached to the top of the shell, is what we eat.

  Fresh *uni* is remarkable—a mustard-colored mass with a subtle, nutlike flavor. Frozen uni can be dreadful. Happily, sea urchins are widely available fresh from waters off both U.S. coasts from August to April, but demand always exceeds supply, and eating sea urchin is an expensive habit.

  Sushi connoisseurs often claim uni as their favorite sushi variety, but most beginners view it with suspicion—the ultimate macho test of the sushi challenge. Attempt uni when you find it fresh and first-rate. If you don't like it right away, consider yourself fortunate. Devotees can run up an appalling bill satisfying their craving for uni.

Tobiko

Masago

- *Tobiko* (flying-fish roe). The roe most commonly served in a sushi bar, after uni and ikura, is probably *tobiko*. These tiny, bright orange eggs are firm and salty, and they almost explode with flavor when you bite them. Tobiko is easy to like and a wonder to look at, particularly when it is enhanced with the bright yellow yolk of a quail egg.

- *Masago* (capelin roe). Capelin is a kind of smelt, and in Japan it is valued particularly for its roe. *Masago* looks and tastes very much like tobiko. It is a slightly lighter orange, though, and a bit tinier than flying-fish roe. It has a fascinating resistance to the bite and a tingly saltiness.

  You may want to compare masago and tobiko bite for bite to discern the subtle difference in their flavors. Although masago is imported to America less often than tobiko, sushi bars with a Japanese clientele are likely to have both.

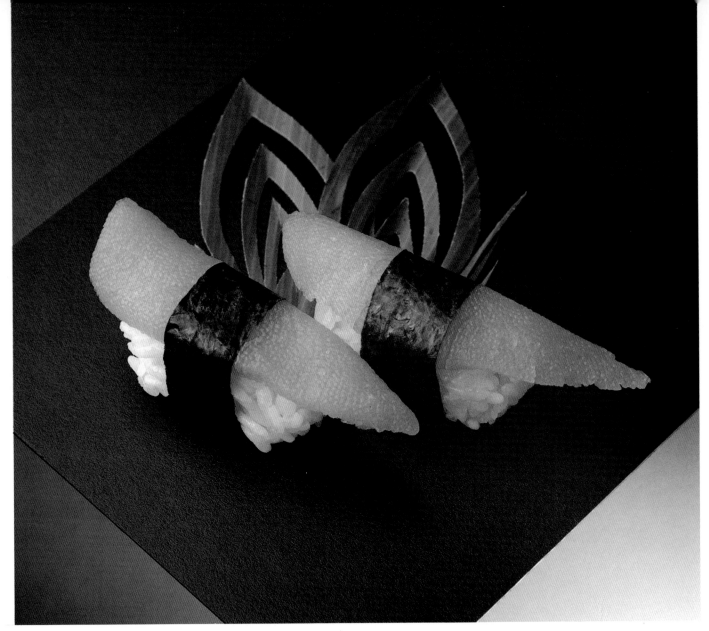

*Kazunoko*

■ *Kazunoko* (herring roe). Herring roe is highly prized by the Japanese as the traditional dish of their New Year's celebration, and its exorbitant price has earned it the name "yellow diamonds." Herring from the San Francisco area are particularly favored by the Japanese because they produce a high yield of roe, and the San Francisco Bay herring run is legendary among commercial fishermen for creating fortunes overnight.

The small silver fish travel in dense schools, following the plankton migrations, and appear in the bay suddenly in incredible profusion. Fishermen trade stories of $50,000 catches, and they respond eagerly to the sudden massive influx of the shiny fish, as do Japanese fish brokers, who wait on the docks with suitcases full of cash. Fishermen also tell stories of nets so full that startled herring, sounding en masse, pulled fishing boats down after them.

The drama of the herring run is astonishing, but no more astonishing than the Japanese passion for *kazunoko.* The little fish itself is high in protein and very tasty, but in Japan it is overlooked in favor of its roe, which is small and so firm as to be almost rubbery. The egg clusters are marinated in sweet sake, broth, and soy sauce, which gives them a golden color, and served whole as nigirizushi.

Occasionally, unmarinated herring roe will appear in the sushi case, the tiny white eggs scattered on green seaweed. It is called *kazunoko konbu* and is served as nigirizushi, in rolled sushi, or as a snack between courses.

*Tamago*

■ *Tamago* (hen's egg omelet). *Tamago* is a firm omelet made in a square pan. Sweetened egg batter is poured in a very thin sheet into the pan. As it cooks, the chef flips it with his chopsticks and rolls it to one side; then he pours in another layer, rolls out the first layer, and repeats the process until the omelet is an inch thick and dense with paper-thin layers. Cooled, it is sliced and served as sushi on a pad of rice bound with a narrow girdle of seaweed, or tucked into a sushi roll with other ingredients. Its sweetness is refreshing between fish sushi courses, or as the conclusion to a meal.

Skillful preparation of tamago is considered one of the high points of a sushi chef's skill, and in Japan, a first-time customer at a sushi bar might order tamago to start. If it is not up to standards, he may leave on the spot, without paying the bill. Such behavior in America, where overcooked scrambled eggs are the rule, might be considered presumptuous.

Makizushi means "rolled sushi" and it is thin strips of fish and vegetables rolled in sushi rice and crisp sheets of seaweed, and then sliced into bite-sized rounds. The seaweed is called *nori,* and another name for makizushi is *norimaki.* Although it doesn't occupy the same exalted position as nigirizushi in Japanese cuisine, it is extremely popular and available in sushi bars everywhere.

Makizushi is a particular favorite among sushi neophytes; in fact, it is most people's introduction to sushi, and it is easy for a beginner to like. The hint of raw tuna in a slice of makizushi is a good way to dispel the notion that uncooked fish is creepy.

At first, the thought of nibbling on makizushi's seaweed wrapper may give you pause, but eating nori is only unnerving till you've tried it. It combines the light, seabreeze taste of seaweed with a crackly texture, and its crisp saltiness complements the soft sweetness of sushi rice.

Nori is made from several species of *Porphyra* seaweed that are washed and spread thin to dry in much the same way that wood pulp is made into paper. Before it is used, nori is toasted to enhance its flavor and texture and turn it a brilliant green.

Makizushi comes in two sizes at the sushi bar. *Hosomaki,* which means "slender roll," is the most familiar. The chef rolls it with a small, flexible bamboo mat. It is about an inch in diameter and contains one or two ingredients plus rice. Hosomaki makes six bite-sized rounds.

You may also ask for *temaki,* "hand roll," which is smaller, loosely rolled by hand and given to you like an ice cream cone to be eaten in two or three bites.

Almost anything can be rolled into makizushi, but there are a few standard varieties that you may want to try.

# M A K I Z U S H I

- *Futomaki* [top row] is makizushi in a class by itself. It is a fat, fancy roll served in Japanese restaurants as lunch or a snack. It is about two inches thick, a sort of Japanese burrito, and has six ingredients inside, including sweet bright pink fish powder, egg, strips of gourd, and other vegetables. The six ingredients are always the same, and the pinwheel effect they make at the center of a slice of *futomaki* is quite impressive. Because it is almost a meal in itself, futomaki is not served at many sushi bars.

- *Tekkamaki* [upper middle row] has fresh raw tuna at the center. *Tekka* is the word for gambling parlors in Japan, where the snack originated as a quick, hand-held food that could be eaten at the gaming table, much as our sandwich was devised by the Earl of Sandwich so he could eat his dinner without interrupting his card game.

- *Kappamaki* [lower middle row] has slivered cucumber, *kyūri,* in the middle and it is a crunchy and refreshing sushi-bar course. It is named after Kappa, a water goblin in Japanese mythology. He was very fond of cucumbers, which he stole from the fields near his riverbank home. Kappa is always pictured with a saucer on his head that looks like a cucumber slice. According to the myths, the saucer must always be kept full of water or Kappa loses his goblin powers.

- *Oshinkomaki* [bottom row] has bright yellow pickled daikon at the center, tastes vinegary, and delivers a lot of crunch.

- *Unakyū* combines grilled freshwater eel and cucumber at the center of a roll.

- *Anakyū* has grilled marine eel and cucumber at the center.

- *Umekyū* is sushi rice rolled with cucumber and *neri ume,* a tart plum paste that clears the palate and leaves a pleasant aftertaste. It is a good way to end a sushi dinner.

In some Japanese restaurants you will come across styles of sushi that are not ordinarily served in sushi bars. They are intended for take-out or picnics or to mark a special occasion. The main ingredient of these kinds of sushi is sushi rice that has been layered, formed, or wrapped in a variety of ways.

- *Saikuzushi* [pictured], or festival sushi, is a decorative kind of norimaki prepared for special occasions. It is an elaborate art form. Rice is tinted different colors, sectioned off with seaweed, and then rolled. When it is sliced, complex images of cranes, flowers, or landscapes appear—beautiful, edible cloisonnés. Like our Christmas fruitcake, though, *saikuzushi* is more often admired than eaten.

- *Oshizushi* is classic Kansai-style sushi. It is sushi rice pressed into a mold with marinated or boiled fish, usually mackerel, on top. It is removed from the mold and cut into sections when it is served.

- *Chirashizushi* means "scattered sushi," and it is sushi rice spread in a box or a bowl with nine kinds of fish and vegetables scattered on top or mixed into the rice, and nine steps in preparation. (Nine is considered the luckiest number by the Japanese.) Each person helps himself to as much as he likes.

- *Chakinzushi* is sushi rice in a yellow egg-crepe wrapper shaped and tied like a lady's drawstring purse. Sometimes a single pea or a small shrimp decorates the ruffled part of the wrapper.

- *Fukusazushi* is sushi rice folded in a thin sheet of yellow egg crepe. *Fukusa* means "silk scarf," and this sushi is named after the fabric squares knotted around gifts or special belongings in Japan.

- *Battera matsumae* is a box lunch in itself. Husbands pick it up on their way home from work in Japan the way an American might stop off for a pizza to take home for dinner. It is made with the leaflike protective covering of the bamboo shoot, tan and papery and nearly two feet long, that is layered with seaweed, a block of sushi rice about the size of a brick, and a large fillet of marinated mackerel. A silken, transparent, pale green seaweed is draped over the top, and the bamboo is folded tightly around everything and tied with knotted strips of leaf. The flavors mingle and improve with age. Before refrigeration, bamboo was used to wrap and preserve fish, and *battera matsumae* keeps well at room temperature for several days.

# KANSAI-STYLE SUSHI

A variety of condiments and garnishes are served with sushi and sashimi to enhance their flavor and embellish their appearance. In many cases, what goes with what is ordained by the tradition and art of the cuisine. A few accompaniments—soy sauce, wasabi, sliced pickled ginger, and daikon—are absolutely fundamental to the taste and appearance of sushi and sashimi. The others you may encounter as you explore the more esoteric offerings of the sushi bar.

- *Shōyu,* "soy sauce," is Japan's most essential seasoning. It is a variation of Chinese soy sauce, but is lighter and less salty, and many sushi bars are proud that they blend their own. *Shōyu* is made of wheat, soybeans, malt seed, and yeast mixed and allowed to ferment for a year. Bottles of shōyu are placed along the countertop in a sushi bar, and a saucer is provided for your use. Pour yourself a small amount, not a bath—drowning sushi or sashimi in soy sauce is a mistake. Already seasoned sushi, such as eel, does not need soy sauce.

- *Gari* is sliced pickled ginger. It is served at the corner of your sushi tray or on the counter, and it is meant to be eaten between sushi courses to refresh the palate. Although the chef will replenish your supply if you ask him, gari should be eaten a slice at a time. It is a garnish, not a salad.

- *Wasabi* is the very pungent green horseradish spread inside most nigirizushi. The vegetable is a knobby green root that grows alongside clear, mountain streams in Japan, and a powdered form is used here, mixed with a few drops of water to make a stiff paste. A pinch of wasabi is served with sashimi for you to mix into your soy sauce. In nigirizushi, however, the chef puts a streak between the rice and the fish, and the sushi is dipped into soy sauce only, not a soy-wasabi combination. If you love wasabi, ask the chef to put more inside. It is strong stuff, and chefs complain that Americans eat it like peanut butter, thinking it demonstrates their bravery. It merely makes them numb.

# ACCOMPANIMENTS

- *Daikon* is a giant white radish served grated, diced, or shredded thin and wispy as a garnish for sashimi. It aids digestion, particularly of fats, and is a refreshing contrast to rich fish. On rare occasions it is used to garnish sushi.

- *Shiso* is a fresh green leaf related to mint, and its taste is a piquant blend of mint and lemon. It is used as a garnish with sashimi, tucked in roe sushi for color, or included in various rolled sushi where its tanginess complements the other ingredients. Shiso is a subtle and delightful surprise.

- *Ponzu* is a citrus-flavored soy sauce often made with lemon juice in America, though in Japan, a sharper-tasting citrus fruit, called *sudachi,* is used. Ponzu contains rice vinegar, sweet sake, and a few other seasonings, and it is served with paper-thin sashimi.

- *Goma,* "sesame seeds," can be either black or white. The black are somewhat stronger in flavor, and both are used for a color accent as well as taste, occasionally on eel and often in rolled sushi.

- *Uzura no tamago* is fresh quail egg. Its shell is brown-and-white speckled and only about an inch long. The egg itself looks just like a miniature chicken egg. It is served raw as a garnish on roe sushi—tobiko, masago, or ikura—and it is worth asking for as much for its sunny appearance as its silky taste.

- *Yamaimo* is a white root known as mountain yam or mountain potato. It is cut into crisp slices as a crunchy accent to roe sushi, or grated and made into a cold porridge and served with a quail egg on top, a dish for the adventurous. It is thought to be an aphrodisiac, and if you request *yamaimo* the chef may ask if you are alone. If you say yes, he may suggest you have it some other time.

- *Baran* is a flat, green plastic garnish shaped like a picket fence. Its use is a reflection of the ancient tradition of wrapping fish in parts of the bamboo plant that contained natural preservatives and kept the fish fresh. As refrigeration made this unnecessary, ti leaves replaced the bamboo and were used as a garnish or as plates for sushi. Fresh greens finally gave way to plastic facsimiles, which are made in a profusion of decorative shapes, but serve no function except ornamentation and nostalgia. They are certainly not meant to be eaten.

■ *Tsukidashi,* "side dishes," are surprise accompaniments to a sushi meal. The chef may lay a few sliced pickles on the countertop or present you with a small dish of slivered, cooked shellfish in vinegar sauce or a fresh cucumber sliced in a spiral or spread like a fan. Between rich orders of sushi, he might offer a cold and briny *yamagobō,* a slender, carrotlike root known in English as burdock. Pick it up with your fingers and eat the fat, tender end first. (Chefs say that Americans eat it backwards.) *Edamame,* a fresh soybean pod with the beans still in it, might be another *tsukidashi.* Pinch the pod so the beans pop out the side, eat them, and leave the empty pod on the counter. The variety of tsukidashi is endless. They are not on the menu; they will probably not show up on the bill; and they cannot be ordered since they are prepared spontaneously by the chef and offered according to whim. If you are known to appreciate the unusual, the chef may present you with these snacks when you least expect it.

The beverages served with sushi—green tea, sake, and beer—are more than mere thirst quenchers. Tea and sake are ancient, and they are as much a part of the Japanese cuisine as fish and rice. They complement the subtle flavors of seafood, and like a perfectly chosen wine, serve to enhance the food, not just wash it down. The light taste of Japanese beer is also considered an excellent foil for the rich taste of sushi.

■ *Ocha* is green tea. Originally used for medicinal purposes, it is considered essential to life in Japan. Because the Japanese diet is so salty, and water is not drunk as such, great quantities of tea are consumed at meals and at every opportunity. Green tea refreshes the palate and is even drinkable alongside sake.

The Japanese traditionally drink only green tea. They consider black tea foreign, although the leaves from both kinds come from the same plant. Fresh leaves for green tea are steamed to destroy an enzyme that would otherwise ferment and cause the leaves to turn black, like the tea of China, India, and England.

In the twelfth century, powdered tea was used by the Zen monks as a stimulant to keep them awake during all-night prayers, and its use flourished along with the Buddhist religion, evolving into the highly ritualized tea ceremony.

Various grades of tea are served in Japan, classified according to the way they are grown and picked. The best and most expensive grades come from the tenderest young leaves harvested from ancient bushes grown only in the shade. The various grades are brewed differently; coarser grades require hotter water. *Sencha,* a high grade of Japanese tea, is served in sushi bars because its taste is particularly good with raw fish.

Japanese tea is always drunk piping hot and without cream or sugar. You are encouraged to slurp it, to suck air in with the tea, which will cool it a bit. In sushi bars, you are apt to hear tea called *agari,* which is sushi slang. It actually means "finished."

# B E V E R A G E S

■ *Sake* is a fragrant, pale gold, faintly sweet rice wine, with a taste similar to good sherry. It is served warm in the winter, cool in the summer, and contains about seventeen percent alcohol (regular wine contains eleven or twelve percent). Sake is not really wine, since grain, not fruit, is its basis, and the fermentation process is similar to that used to make beer. It goes well with all Japanese food, particularly fish, and every sort of occasion. According to Japanese notions, there is no dish, except the honorable bowl of plain rice at the end of a meal, that isn't enhanced by sake. It is potent despite its gentle flavor, and some say its warmth makes it all the more intoxicating.

Sake is brought to the table in small porcelain bottles, *tokkuri,* and poured into tiny cups, *sakazuki.* The host pours for his guest, then the guest for the host. It is considered a gesture of friendship to keep a companion's cup filled, and when sake is being poured for you, hold up your cup to acknowledge the courtesy. One does not refuse more sake even if rather drunk. If you must refuse, turn your empty cup over or your host will continue to fill it despite your protestations, thinking you are being coy.

Although almost always served warm, during the hot summer months sake may be served cold from square cedar boxes called *masu,* an ancient unit of measure. Salt is placed in one corner and the whole cup downed in a single gulp like tequila. Regular customers keep their own masu at the sushi bar, identified by their teeth marks.

Most of the year, sake is heated to about body temperature by placing the serving bottle in a pan of hot water. Many sushi bars have machines for heating sake, given to them by sake vendors. They are convenient, but they keep the wine at a uniform temperature that is usually too hot.

For good sake, high-quality new rice and pure water from mountain streams are required. Certain locales in Japan produce superior sake because they are blessed with one or the other. Steamed white rice is inoculated with a special mold and allowed to ferment. It takes six weeks to two months to produce, and is drunk right away. There is no aging process, and there are no vintage years. Some think sake is best drunk within three months of bottling. Sake is either sweet or dry: sweetness is its natural condition, dryness is created artificially. There are numerous brands available in Japan, all quite good, and the proprietor of a sushi shop usually chooses just one to serve his customers. In the United States, imported sake is available, but most American sushi bars serve domestically produced sake, which is made according to traditional methods and is considered to be very good.

Sake comes in three grades. *Tokkyū,* "premium class," is the best and usually only served on special occasions. *Ikkyū,* "first class," is really second class, but still excellent. *Nikyū,* "second class," is a popular and very drinkable third class. Standards are high for every grade of sake, and even third-grade brands are very good.

The Japanese lead a high-pressure existence by virtue of their crowded cities, competitive business climate, and rigid culture. When they do relax, it is with abandon, and drinking sake with friends and associates is almost a nightly endeavor for most businessmen. It is no disgrace to be drunk in Japan. The low-fat diet somehow allows the alcohol to take effect almost at once and the Japanese become pink-cheeked, friendly, and extremely loquacious rather quickly.

Sake does not have the numbing effect on the taste buds that hard liquor seems to; its taste enhances rather than destroys flavors, and its heady effect contributes to the vitality at a sushi bar.

■ *Bīru* means "beer," and several Japanese varieties are served in sushi bars, all of excellent quality. Kirin has a rich, nutlike flavor. Asahi is the sweetest, closest to the taste of American beer. Sapporo is more bitter and lighter, like European beer. Beer has a clean, refreshing quality that goes well with sushi, and if you are a beer fancier, you should sample all three brands.

The Japanese are great believers in learning through apprenticeship. They feel a skill perfected through years of repetition has a transcendent nature, and that only by working alongside a master can a student absorb and understand a craft and the values behind it. Sushi chefs, *shokunin,* begin their training as delivery boys and dishwashers in the sushi bar, working their way up to cleaning fish and washing rice. It is only after several years of this discipline that they are permitted to pick up a knife. It may be ten years before they have earned the position of head chef.

The sushi chef is an heir to the samurai tradition. The samurai were at once soldiers and scholars, gentlemen of high personal standards and unshakable self-discipline, with no use for self-indulgence. Chefs uphold an ideal they call *inase,* a snappy, clean-cut kind of machismo. They wear spotless jackets, and often sport no-nonsense crew cuts and *hajimaki,* the knotted headband that samurai wore to indicate they were prepared for battle. For the sushi chef, it is a mark of style, evidence that he is serious about his work.

The chef's day is long. He is at the market first thing in the morning, then in the shop hours before it opens, busy with preparation. Kitchen helpers are not permitted to make sushi rice, and only the chef chooses the day's fish. He may serve lunch as well as dinner and will be on his feet well into the night, keeping a demanding, if appreciative, audience fed and entertained. A good chef is unshakable under fire, gracious as well as deft. He possesses a calm self-assurance that never betrays fatigue or irritation. It is a matter of pride that goes beyond professionalism. It is a matter of honor.

The sushi bar is no place for an amateur. Recently, the sudden popularity of sushi bars in the United States has given rise to a crop of instant chefs, cooks trained almost overnight to slice sashimi and serve sushi with great flair. Many of these chefs, often those with the flashiest style, have learned the technical skills, but lack the self-discipline that comes with years of apprenticeship. They are referred to as "noodle chefs," and never attain the status of a properly trained shokunin, even though their American customers may never discern the difference.

Japanese cooking is a visual cuisine. At certain imperial banquets, court etiquette demands that guests be content to merely look at the food, and *katachi no aji*—"the flavor of the shape"—is often referred to. A sushi chef is regarded as an artist. Cooking as a profession is highly regarded in Japan (in Buddhist monasteries, only the highest initiates are allowed to prepare food), and a good chef, like a samurai warrior, is autonomous. He can pick up his knives and go anywhere he chooses.

# THE SUSHI CHEF

A sushi chef's knives are as important to him as a sword to a samurai, and the two have much in common. The ancient art of Japanese sword making produced perhaps the finest blade in history, and the same techniques are used today to forge knives of incredibly hard carbon steel. A carbon-steel blade can be honed to so sharp an edge that it can literally split a hair. Far superior to stainless steel, it dulls slowly and can be brought back easily if cared for. Japanese knives are sharpened by hand with a whetstone, never a steel or grinding wheel, and whetstones from particular quarries are known for their compatibility with certain knives. A sushi chef has his own set of knives, which cost several hundred dollars apiece. He sharpens them before and after use, wipes them clean every few strokes, wraps them carefully every night, and stores them in a special place away from other tools that might chip the blade. Some chefs even take their knives home at night to ensure that nothing happens to them.

Most Japanese knives are sharpened on one side of the blade only, unlike Western knives, where two sharpened surfaces meet in a V. A single-edged blade cuts faster and more cleanly than a double-edged one. On a Japanese knife, the cutting edge is always on the right side, because most Japanese are right-handed. (Until very recently, left-handed children were set straight early in life.) Japanese chefs primarily use three knives:

■ *Sashimi bōchō* are long, slender knives with seven- to fifteen-inch blades. They are used for slicing sashimi. The pointed style, *yanagiba* [left], is from Ōsaka; the blunt-tipped style, *takobiki* [second from left], is from Tōkyō. These are the knives most used by sushi chefs for cutting fish into perfect cubes and slices.

■ *Usuba bōchō* [center] is a vegetable knife. The cutting edge is straight, the back edge curves, and this knife resembles our meat cleaver but is much lighter. It is used for paring and cutting vegetables and is so efficient in the right hands that it can be faster than a food processor.

■ *Deba bōchō* [right and far right] are basically fish knives. They have seven- to twelve-inch blades that are straight along the edge and curved along the back. They seem very heavy by Western standards, but are considered extremely versatile by the Japanese, who prefer to use a light touch and a heavy knife, letting the weight of the knife do the work.

# TOOLS

There are three basic strokes in Japanese carving:

- *Hiki giri* is the drawing cut. The chef allows the weight of his knife to do the work, while drawing it toward him. It is used mainly with the *sashimi bōchō* for slicing fish.

- *Oshi giri* is a pushing cut—the center of the blade is pushed straight down. It is used to cut through seaweed without making ragged edges and to slice makizushi without pulling it apart.

- *Tsuku giri* is a forward-thrusting cut. When the *usuba bōchō* is used to cut through raw foods—in dicing cucumber, for example—this cut is used.

Sushi chefs prefer a cutting board, *manaita,* that is all one piece with the grain running the length of the board. Cypress is the most commonly used wood, although willow is also excellent. The board must be hard, but have just the slightest amount of give as the knife passes through the fish. Laminated wood is rejected as having an uneven resistance and a tendency to split.

What is being cut is always held lightly but firmly with the left hand. The knife blade is never raised above the height of the knuckles, both for the preservation of the maximum number of fingers and to establish a good rhythm.

After years of apprenticeship, the chef's knife becomes an extension of his hand. Slicing fish paper thin, cutting a cucumber so it unfolds like an accordion or opens like a fan appear to be effortless feats. An experienced chef can slice a cucumber rapid-fire and so thin you can see through it, while he carries on a conversation with you, all the while looking you in the eye.

Eventually you may want to prepare sushi at home, if only to tide you over on the night when your favorite sushi bar is closed. You can learn a great deal about technique from watching your chef, although he will make it look easier than it is.

■ *Rice* is the common denominator of all sushi, and a proper batch of rice is the pride of every Japanese cook. Faithful adherence to the recipe will guarantee you perfect results, provided you start with the right ingredients. Our familiar long-grained rice will not do. It cooks up dry and separate, and it is impossible to eat with chopsticks or form into sushi pads. The Japanese use short-grained rice, which clings together nicely and has the satisfying chewy texture sushi gourmets love. It is available in Oriental markets.

To make sushi rice, you will need a three-quart heavy-bottomed pot with a tight-fitting lid, a wooden bowl, a spatula, and something to use as a fan. You may want to own a *shamoji,* the broad wooden paddle used in Japan to mix the rice, or a Japanese paper fan, although a shirt cardboard or folded newspaper will do as well. Ultimately, you may wish to purchase a gas or electric rice cooker, available in Japanese stores. These take the guesswork out of rice cooking.

# M A K I N G  Y O U R  O W N  S U S H I

Japanese cooks sometimes vary the following recipe by adding a tablespoon of sake to the rice water, or changing the amounts of sugar and vinegar to suit their tastes. Dried, packaged *konbu,* "kelp," is available in Japanese markets along with regular rice vinegar and *sushi su,* a rice vinegar made just for sushi rice and already flavored with salt, sugar, and MSG.

| | |
|---|---|
| *2 cups short-grained rice* | *1 tablespoon sugar* |
| *2 cups water* | *2 teaspoons salt* |
| *¼ cup rice vinegar* | *3" square of konbu* |

Thoroughly rinse the rice until the water runs clear, about five minutes, and let it drain in a colander for an hour. Usually, Japanese rice is coated with a cereal powder that must be washed off, even though the package may say it isn't necessary. When the rice is cleaned, put it into the pot. Clean the seaweed with a damp cloth and cut fringe into one side to help release the flavor. Bury it in the rice. Add the water, cover, and bring to a boil over high heat. Remove the seaweed just as the water boils or it will flavor the rice too strongly. Reduce the heat to medium and cook for five minutes, then reduce to low and cook for fifteen minutes without removing the lid, even for a peek. When the rice makes a dry crackly sound, remove it from the heat and let it stand covered for another ten minutes.

While the rice is cooking, combine the salt, sugar, and vinegar in a small saucepan. Heat and stir the mixture till the sugar is dissolved, then allow it to cool.

Turn the rice out into a shallow wooden bowl. The wood helps absorb the moisture. Do not use anything metal, as it may react with the vinegar and create a bad taste. Add the vinegar dressing a little at a time, cutting it into the rice with the rice paddle or spatula [1]. Use a horizontal motion to keep from bruising the soft rice grains as they cool. Every so often, dip the spoon into cold water to keep the rice from sticking to it. While you're stirring the rice with one hand, cool it with a fan held in the other, which will make it glossy [2]. An electric fan or a live assistant makes this process easier. It takes about ten minutes either way.

Sushi rice can be kept for several hours at room temperature, covered with a damp cloth. It should not be refrigerated and should be eaten the same day it is made. When you are ready to make the sushi pads, have a little bowl of vinegar water (one-third vinegar, two-thirds water) ready to dip your fingers into to keep the rice from sticking to them. Put a couple of tablespoons of rice into your right hand and press it firmly into an oval shape, using the first two fingers of your left hand [3,4]. Remember, this little maneuver only took the chef a couple of years to perfect.

RICE

1

3

2

4

1

2

3

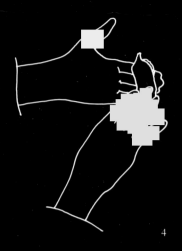

4

5

6

■ *Nigirizushi* can be made with almost any freshly caught saltwater fish, shellfish, or high-quality processed roe. Find yourself an excellent fish market and learn to recognize freshness and quality in all of these items.

When selecting a fish, look it in the eyes. They should be clear and bright, never cloudy. The gills should be bright red inside and the whole fish should smell fresh as a sea breeze, have no trace of sliminess, and be resilient to the touch.

Although the sushi chef buys his fish whole, you will probably want to have your selections cleaned, skinned, and filleted for you. One pound of cleaned fish will make two dozen sushi, and serve eight to twelve people as appetizers, four for a main meal. Keep it chilled until the last possible moment. Then place the fish on a cutting board, and with a very sharp knife cut the fillet across the grain into quarter-inch-thick slices, then trim them to form one-by-two-inch sections.

Pick up the fish morsel with your left hand, holding it gently between thumb and forefinger, and hold a rice pad in your right hand [1]. Brush a streak of wasabi (buy it powdered in an Oriental market) down the center of the fish slice with your right forefinger [2]. Cradle the fish slice in your left hand and press the rice pad into it [3]. Then roll the sushi, fish side up, onto your fingers [4] and press in the top and sides to firm its shape [5]. Place it on the serving tray [6].

Clams should be bought when they are tightly closed to be sure they are alive. Clams with protruding siphons will constrict somewhat when touched, indicating they are still alive and fresh. If you dig clams yourself, be sure to obey quarantine laws during the summer months. They are for your protection, not the clam's. Cover the clams with salted water and let them stand for fifteen minutes to rid them of sand, which will settle to the bottom of the bucket. Change the water and let the clams stand several times until no more sand appears.

Open and scoop small clams from their shells and rinse them in cold salted water and drain. Clams may be sliced nearly in half and spread open, butterflied, for a thinner and more manageable sushi. With large clams, open the shell and remove the body. Cut away the digestive organs, leaving the firm, meaty muscle. Slice the muscle thinly and add salt, massage well, then rinse under cold water. Score the slices with a sharp knife to make them more tender. Clams are pressed onto sushi rice as above.

Shrimp is very popular in sushi bars, and although raw shrimp is considered a great delicacy, it is not recommended unless the shrimp are purchased live and from pure waters. Most shrimp sold in the United States are frozen and should be cooked. If you do find fresh shrimp for sale, they should be firm, with tight-fitting shells, and should smell fresh. A stale shrimp has the smell of ammonia, and if even one smells bad, the whole batch is on its way out.

# MAKIZUSHI

1

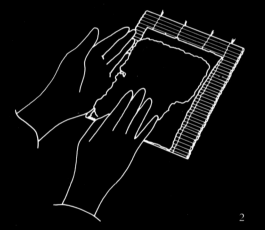

2

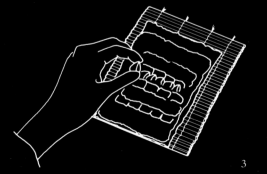

3

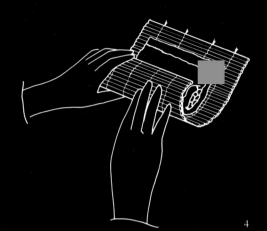

4

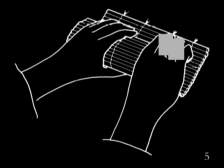

5

6

To cook shrimp, devein them, and leaving the shells on, skewer them on toothpicks to prevent them from curling as they cook. Drop them into boiling salted water to which you have added a dash of rice vinegar. Boil the shrimp for three minutes, until they turn opaque and pink, then plunge them into cold water. Remove the toothpicks and peel the shrimp, leaving the tails on for decoration. Split each down the underside, taking care not to cut all the way through. Spread open into a butterfly shape, and press the shrimp onto a rice pad as you did with sliced fish.

To make roe sushi, or any gunkan-style nigirizushi, toast a sheet of nori seaweed (available in cellophane packages in Japanese markets) over an open flame until it turns a bright green. Cut it into one-by-six-inch strips and wrap each one around a rice pad, sealing the band with a bit of smashed rice. Spoon in roe, bits of fish or shellfish, and garnish with a sprinkle of lemon juice, a dot of wasabi, or a fresh quail egg.

To make two dozen salmon roe sushi, you will need two four-ounce jars of salmon roe and four or five sheets of nori. Seaweed loses its crispness quickly, so this type of sushi should be made just before serving.

■ *Makizushi* is a bit easier to make than nigirizushi. You will need a bamboo rolling mat, available in Japanese stores, plus sushi rice, nori seaweed, and whatever ingredients you want to put inside—sliced cucumbers, bits of fish, pickled vegetables.

Toast a sheet of nori as for gunkan-style nigirizushi. Then place it on the bamboo mat, shiny side down [1]. The mat should lie so it rolls away from you, not from side to side. Keeping your hands moistened with vinegar water, put two or three tablespoons of sushi rice in the center of the nori and spread evenly, about three-eighths inch thick, over the seaweed [2]. Use the palm of your free hand at the side of the seaweed to form a firm edge, and leave a one-inch margin at the top of the nori to seal the roll. Spread a streak of wasabi across the middle, then add layers of fish and vegetables across the center of the rice [3].

To roll, fold the bamboo mat so the filling is enclosed in the center of the nori [4]. Press the mat around the roll for about thirty seconds to shape it [5], then moisten the margin of seaweed and seal the roll as tightly as possible. The most difficult part of making makizushi is getting the roll tight enough to prevent it from disintegrating when it's sliced.

Remove the mat from around the roll, press in the loose ends and place it on a cutting board, seam side down. Slice the roll into one-inch rounds, using a wet, sharp knife [6]. Do not saw, but cut firmly, straight down, or the roll will come apart. Turn the slices rice side up for decorative effect.

As your addiction to sushi flourishes, you may be called upon by your trust officer to justify your expenses or your bowling league to explain your absence. If a fantastic new health regimen would impress either of them, here are the facts to back you up.

The Japanese are generally healthier than Americans. Their incidence of heart disease is about half ours; and breast cancer, thought to be related to a high-fat diet, is nonexistent. When they emigrate to the United States and adopt our eating habits, their rate of heart disease and breast cancer parallels our own.

The Japanese have never been great meat eaters. In early days, cows and horses were forbidden as food because they were more useful as tractors. When Buddhism flourished in the eighth century, eating meat was discouraged for religious reasons, and there has never been enough arable land to support much grazing. The staples of the Japanese diet are rice, fish, and soybeans. The Japanese consume over half the world's fish catch, and derive the balance of their protein from soybeans imported from the United States. (We feed this nutritious, cheap, versatile food to livestock.) Vegetable oils are used in cooking. As a result, very little animal fat is consumed, for seafoods are generally much lower in fat than meat, and the fat they do contain is mostly unsaturated. If eaten several times a week, seafood will actually help neutralize the harmful saturated fats from other foods in the diet and reduce body cholesterol. In general, fish and shellfish are fifteen to twenty-five percent protein. Lean fish contain less than five percent fat, the fattiest eel is just twenty percent fat. Porterhouse steak, on the other hand, offers less than twenty percent protein and is forty-two percent fat.

# N U T R I T I O N

Few Japanese are fat. Those who are find themselves congratulated for being so prosperous, for how else could they afford to eat so much and work so little? From a weight watcher's point of view, sushi is the perfect food. The leaner fish contain fewer than 100 calories per 100 grams. The fattiest varieties, mackerel, eel, tuna, still have fewer than 200, while chicken, thought by dieters to be calorically austere, has 250 calories and steak has 500 calories, both per 100 grams. Even cooked rice contains only 100 calories per 100 grams, and a relatively small amount is used for sushi. Sake, on the other hand, contains 239 calories per cup, and don't kid yourself about how many cups you can drink during a modest sushi dinner.

As well as being high in protein and low in fat, fish is extremely easy to digest, even more so when it is eaten raw, and sashimi is often the first thing served in Japanese hospitals to patients who have been on liquid diets.

Seafoods have always been considered to be aphrodisiacs by the Japanese. Although this position has not yet been substantiated by the AMA, most sushi lovers will testify to the sensuality engendered by an evening at a sushi bar.

Although seaweed may seem a strange food to the western palate, it has the remarkable property of being able to sustain life in times of starvation. Seawater contains all the elements in human blood in precisely the same proportions, and it has actually been used for transfusions with excellent results when the real thing was unavailable. Foods from the sea provide a naturally well-balanced diet, rich in vitamins, minerals, and trace elements often missing from land-harvested foods, and seaweed in particular has the ability to absorb these nutrients and pass them along intact.

It is ironic that just when Westerners are discovering the virtues of authentic Japanese cuisine, the Japanese are becoming enamored of the products of American affluence: hamburgers, fast food, and the fattiest beef in the world. There is a recent phenomenon in Japan, *himanji,* fat children who have fallen victim to the availability of junk food, noodles, and the ubiquitous American hamburger. May we catch up with them before they catch up with us.

Your chef may take you more seriously if you attempt to order sushi in Japanese. The language is fairly easy for a beginner to pronounce, and the Japanese are very generous about shabby accents. They believe their language, with its profusion of polite forms, is too difficult for Americans to learn and are delighted at any attempt you make to order or respond in their language.

Japanese contains far fewer sounds than English, and they are pronounced the same way every time, with a crisp, clean accent and all syllables stressed equally. Once you have a feel for how the language is pronounced, you can read it off a menu with impunity.

There are seventeen consonants, and they are pronounced pretty much as you would expect: *b, ch, d, f, g, h, j, k, m, n, p, r, s, sh, t, ts,* and *z*. However, *g* is always hard, as in *go; r* is flapped, staccato, the way the British say *very; f* is a soft, breathy sound somewhere between *f* and *h*; and double consonants require a slight pause to indicate that a letter was doubled, or you may sound like you said another word.

There are five vowels and they are pronounced only one way: *a* as in *father; e* as in *pen; i* as in *machine; o* as in *go; u* as in *soup*. In some words, the vowel may be long, marked with the same sign used to indicate our long vowel sound, but in Japan it simply means that the sound is held longer. In words where two vowels are together, they are each pronounced separately.

It is difficult for Americans to get used to the absence of accent in Japan. All syllables are stressed more or less the same, with changes in pitch taking the place of accent, and often changing the entire meaning of a word. Careful listening should be your guide.

Remember that many sushi chefs are trying to learn English, and are as pleased to know the English name for something as you are the Japanese. The language lessons can be part of the fun of eating sushi.

A   QUICK   JAPANESE   LESSON

Here are a few things to memorize, if you're inclined to paste things on the bathroom mirror:

| | |
|---|---|
| *Konbanwa* | Good evening |
| *Sumimasen* | Excuse me |
| *Itadakimasu* | Bon appetit |
| *Kanpai* | To your health |
| *Dōmo* | Thank you |
| *Arigatō* | Thank you (informal) |
| *Arigatō gozaimashita* | Thank you very much (at the end of an evening) |
| *Kyō wa nani ga oishii desu ka?* | What is good today? |
| *Ika o kudasai* | Please give me squid |
| *Maguro o kudasai* | Please give me tuna |
| *Okanjō* | Bill, check |
| *Oyasumi nasai* | Good night |

In Japan, sushi bars have their own slang. You are likely to hear it used by your chef, but may want to get to know him before slinging around his lingo. *Murasaki* means "purple," and it is sushi slang for soy sauce. *Namida,* "tears," indicates wasabi, also shortened as *sabi. Gyoku* means "jewel," and it is a name for tamago. *Agari* means "finished," and indicates tea. *Sabinuki* means "no wasabi, please." *Oaiso* means "the check."

In no time, you will think of your favorite sushi by its Japanese name, and to ask for it in English would seem as out of place as ordering a milkshake. Nobody will think less of you if you can't manage Japanese right away, but food ordered in the native tongue always seems to taste better.

# I N D E X

*Mia Detrick* grew up in Claremont, California, and graduated from Pomona College with a degree in writing. She served as a guest college editor at *Mademoiselle* magazine in 1965 and now owns two stores, a clothing boutique and a flower shop, in Mill Valley, California. Her love of the ocean and absorption with Japanese culture led her to write this book.

*Kathryn Kleinman* received a bachelor of fine arts degree from the University of Minnesota, where she studied painting and drawing. She is a commercial photographer based in San Francisco.